T0365342

VIRAL
SPIRAL

A COLLECTION OF CHILLING POEMS AND PHOTOS
ABOUT COVID-19 AND BLACK LIVES MATTER

SARAH P. ROSS

Copyright © 2020 by Sarah P. Ross.816963

All rights reserved. No part of this book may
be reproduced or transmitted in any form or by
any means, electronic or mechanical, including
photocopying, recording, or by any information storage
and retrieval system, without permission in writing from
the copyright owner.

Any people depicted in stock imagery provided by
Pixabay Images are models, and such images are
being used for illustrative purposes only.
Certain stock imagery © Pixabay Images.

To order additional copies of this book, contact:
Xlibris
844-714-8691
www.Xlibris.com
Orders@Xlibris.com

ISBN: Softcover   978-1-6641-2815-6
        Hardcover   978-1-6641-2816-3
        EBook   978-1-6641-2814-9

Library of Congress Control Number: 2020916746

Print information available on the last page

Rev. date: 10/27/2020

CONTENTS

FOREWORD

The pandemic of our lifetime, the era of Covid-19, was a time of mystery, death, and fear as never before seen. It revealed the nurse's face imprinted red as she cried behind her mask and the EMT loading soon-to-be-dead onto the ambulance. Amidst the Food Bank's love and sustenance was news of Captain Crozier's termination, fired for trying to save his men from Covid's annihilation. Even Governor Cuomo acted as the surrogate president as New Yorkers clapped from their windows to thank first responders for their magic, and people stayed home, always to celebrate alone.

It was just the time when nothing made sense and everything reeked of false pretense. It was a time when working for gratuity changed to delivery, when jobs were all gone and bills pilled overwhelmingly high! Stocks plummeted radically. Another Depression was nigh. Drugs became the crutch for each hour, and abuse of all sorts ruled rampid with power. There is no escape when one's quarantined; children learned a way of life not meant to be. Nursing homes hid the dead bodies of their residents, while all people of color died disproportionately. The meat-packers were forced to work against their own will; Native Americans once again, by a virus, were killed. The homeless had to endure even more suffering, but for the first time, from Coronavirus, our air became clean.

George Floyd started his own pandemic for the BLACK LIVES MATTER task as the president gassed peaceful protestors to clear a path, never wearing a mask, his followers to never dare ask. The virus continued to baffle and control as Americans writhed from its pain. The world had changed. All had changed. Yet graduates, though masked, pretended all was the same. Wearing masks, they flung hats up with glee, while uncaring asymptomatics spread the virus epidemically. Monuments of hate and slavery came toppling down, and the sound of protest continued to erupt. A child's birthday was celebrated by her black daddy being gunned down, where he only awkwardly slept.

The bounty of our soldiers rages with this virus today. It is no surprise that innocent children are being caged. "Live and let die" dictated the day that we all blindly march in Corona's parade.

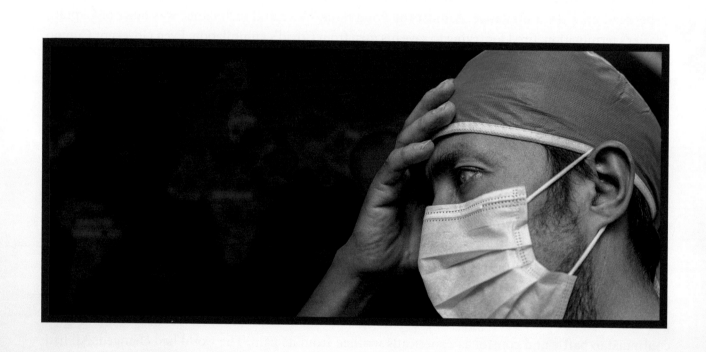

THE NURSE

I am a nurse to save l ives, not this.
Amidst the need for more ventilators,
COVID-19 winning its death kiss.
People so scared, they don't want to die.
No one allowed to visit, or be by their side.
No one allowed in, it's now up to me.
We staff will be their family.
Who I'm here to save, I must just watch die.
This pain is so great, I can't stop one more cry.
One more shift of this hell, lives counting on me.
But am I safe from this virus?
Too much need to just flee.
And will I bring this virus home to my family?
The air I must breath is so hot from this mask.
I'm told I'm lucky to have one, to reuse it, and don't ask.
It has rubbed my face raw and imprinted it red;
The look of a hero is what they have said.
I am an essential worker, the front line of defense.
I must keep on going, though none of this makes sense.

THE EMT

Another call, another call
Back and again you must go
"Why, you cry, is coronavirus all that I know?"
Nightmare of sorrows
Can't breathe, they can't breathe
Another ride to another hospital
Even voluntarily for free.
To stay up all night
You do not care
The urgent need just won't stop
To sleep you don't dare.
Another call, another call
Back and again you must go
Will you also catch this virus
You don't know.
You hold their cold hand
The most you can do
So feeble and frail
It's unfair it's not flu.
Flashing lights and sirens is all you see and hear
Another trip, another hospital
Arriving again near.
You've been told many won't make it
People are dropping like flies
But they're all precious people
That's why that you try
As you rescue another
And pray they don't die!

THE FOOD BANK

A day's work for a loaf of bread
First-world hunger
Cry it's time for the dead.
Covid-19 food lines
Miles are in sight
Children starving by the millions
No school for hunger to fight.
Farmers' crops rotting
Work too low to compete
Crops left to die
When mankind's in defeat.
Sighs come from the children
Hunger grinds them with pain
Parents strain from predictions
Uncertainty driving them insane.
Food first time rationed
U–S it's not there
With nothing to eat
Thank God people care!

WATCHMAN AND THE VIRUS

I am Coronavirus
Destroying the life that has been
I've come to fool the Watchman
Who'll not know when I begin.
Death is all around me
I wanted it this way
But the Watchman's never ready
That's what people say
So I am free to pillage
Raising death tolls every day.
Thousands at a time
A day does not go by
It's amazing what I've accomplished
When I barely even try.
The Watchman says we've got this
With ventilators just not there
Tests and protection rationed
It seems the Watchman doesn't care.
I'm grateful for the Watchman
He cares more for his name
So I will keep on killing
'Cause this is our sick game.

CROZIER OUR HERO

It's Memorial Day again
But this one's not the same
Covid-19 has invaded
In our land this is no game.
The enemy's inside us
So to test is our new call
To be strong to fight this
'Cause Coronavirus attacks us all.
But stats reports to leaders
I'm told is what we must hush
To see the carnage from this
Makes my sad heart crush.
Platoons and VAs loaded
With high cases to ignore
But no one is answering
The cry at our nation's door.
Except for those like Crozier
Who sacrificed to save his men
Who were dying from this virus
On his ship contained within.
They removed him like a martyr
And defamed his precious name
At that moment I saw it happen
Shame's what we all became.

GOVERNOR CUOMO

The surrogate president of the U. S. of A.
The nation's need for a savior
Near noon of each day.
To be honest and reliant
Is what you have sworn
For the love of all Americans
Who have been so horrifically torn.
You have stood by our sides
A true leader to the end
You have stood by your convictions
And never did bend.
We love you, Governor Cuomo
New York's leader for us all
You made do with no real help
To make sure we'd not fall.
What would we have done without you
Our leader in this era of pain?
Coronavirus may have tried us
But with you, we'll rise again!

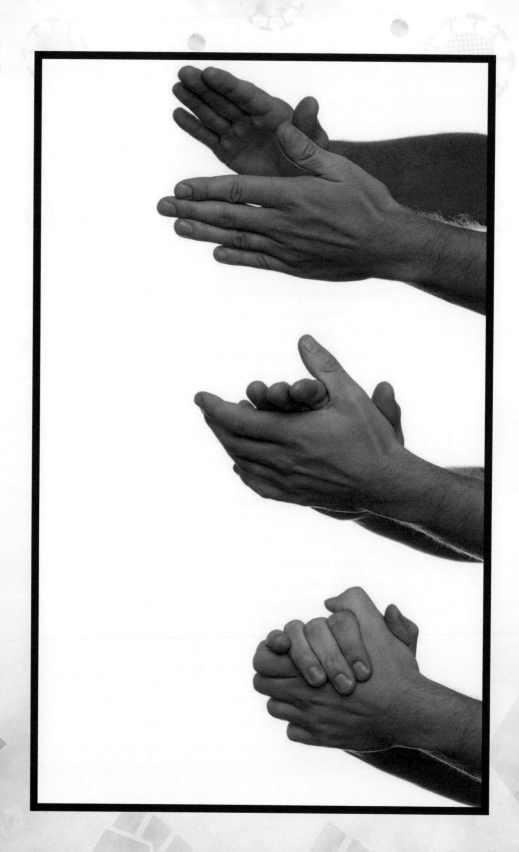

NY CLAPPED

The city that bustles is now stopped every day
Amidst deafening silence, isolation's the way.
Because of a virus quarantining us all
Testing our best to step up for the call
Killing the weakest who must senselessly fall
Forcing all over Covid's death wall.
In the quiet of the evening at 7:00 p.m.
Something magical and eventful always begins.
Hands clap from the windows
From one to another
A chain of love and appreciation like no other.
Out the windows all New Yorkers
Start clapping along
To thank all responders
Even when their strength was all gone.
People getting through this together
When love is what's won
People overcoming this pandemic
Forever, New York strong!

STAY HOME

Isolation due to Covid-19
Has altered our lives substantially.
A baby will die if it's not held
No one's touched me for weeks
I'm a nut in a shell.
Depression is the emotion for every hour
They drag by so slow, draining me of all power.
My hair is a mess, can't go to the salon
Oh well, no one sees
Unless masked I leave home.
Today is the day I'm to celebrate
As I look out my window
For this once-a-year date.
To my surprise, as loved ones drive by
Tears come to my eyes
To hear their sweet cries.
It's for them I stay in
This long quarantine
I'll stay in to defeat Covid-19.

CACKLING CORONAVIRUS

Coronavirus everywhere
Even on TV
Kooky changes in daily care
Each not so funny.
A virus to rule the way for each day
Forbidding to gather, to swim, dance, or pray.
Shelves are so barren
Little meat is in sight
And the worst that could happen
No toilet paper to wipe!
The stocks have all crashed
No jobs for the bills
My ambition is trashed
Thank God for my pills!
Alcohol and drugs are the thrill for each hour
I can't control this virus
But with these, I feel power.
Home schooling's a mess
The kids just won't learn
It's so hard juggling teaching
While doing my perm.
Masks on TV
Are the norm for each day
Broadcasts come from home
Each done their own way.
Sports have no fans
They're not allowed in
There'll be no loud cheers
When the victor does win.
All of this shows
That Covid-19 knows
How to laugh at our highs
And scoff at our lows.
Will a vaccine help
As this virus explodes
Alas, to drive coronavirus
To its cackling close!

THE TIP SERVANT

Once a waiter dependent on gratuity
For now, that way of living is gone.
I used to live fun on my personality
Now close contact is considered wrong.
Social distancing has destroyed my job
A joy of which Covid-19 did rob.
So now I have learned to deliver takeout
To smile and do this with no pout.
The people I deliver to are so very kind
All they want is to support me and finally unwind.
I don't know if this business will survive
But I know that it makes me feel I'm alive.
I hope this pandemic will not destroy my game
'Cause to be a tip servant is what I became.

THE BILLS

What happened to my job
It's no longer there
Coronavirus took it all
Does our leader care?
No money for the bills
Can't even buy us food
Will we end up homeless
The prognosis looks no good.
What about my family
They each depend on me
How do I tell them
Now's the way it must be.
Unemployment on the way
But it is not here yet
I wait for it each day
Today is it I bet.
But bills are very piled
With no real plan in sight
Hell, I know I filed
I'm going crazy from this fight!
Even if this check comes
What good will it do
Because after it's gone
The bills won't be through.
To live on the edge
Day after day
Is pushing me over
Help me, I pray!

THE TRADER

Rushing through my veins
It's money that I crave
I live for the gains
To which I'm a slave.
Stocks up and down
A game I must play
But Covid commands me
At the opening of each day.
A country turned on its head
Another depression to dread
But just as with all
I must toss in this bed.
Speculation fluctuation
Up and down
Life savings on the line
No one makes a sound.
Unemployment levels
Too high to ignore
It's clear from this virus
Nothing will ever be as before.
Businesses closed due to isolation
The world suffering together
For the first time as one
Bare the era of the pandemic
Alas, has begun.

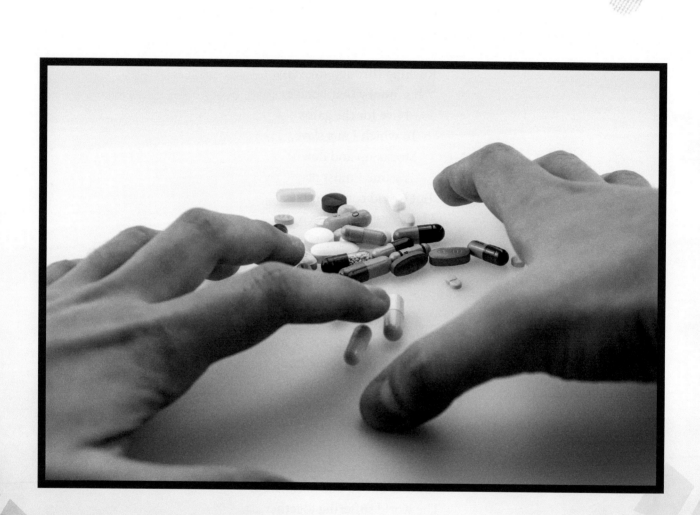

THE TRICK MEDIC

I am your drugs
You must stay home with me.
Together we'll be free
Covid says you can't flee.
I'm here for you each day
I want to play and play.
But your pain deep inside
Is why that I try.
I must suck you dry
Every time that you cry.
To help is my lie
I'll be glad if you die.
But with me, you keep going
Without even knowing.
What is this time
When sense has no rhyme.
So you keep using with me
Your true friend indeed.
To survive this pandemic
With me, the Trick Medic.

THE ABUSED

Quarantined with my abuser
Due to Covid-19
They now feel like a loser
No job, no food, no money.
Come here, bitch
I hear the call
To hit me again
'Til I must fall.
"Help!" I cry
As blood drips down my skin
People say to stay home
But it's not safe to be in.
Domestic violence strengthened
Without any ease
Just get me out of this place
Immediately!
Coronavirus has trapped me
Must I stay in this place
As my abuser takes advantage
And pummels my face!

MY NURSERY RHYME

Is there a world for me
I'm only a kid
I shouldn't see what I see
Of this virus Covid.
My parents are not themselves
They drink all the time
With many fighting spells
They think this is fine.
Hunger seems to stay
The pain won't go away
There is no school to learn
And no friends so I can play.
Fire's on TV
The world is turned inside
There seems no hope for me
So I choose to hide.
Slapped abusively
There is nowhere to run
All I now know is this
Inside's where I call home.
But when I look outside
At the world that I behold
The question on my mind
Is will I ever yet grow old.
In this Covid time
Life's ladder, I will climb
Past my parents' secret crimes
For this is my nursery rhyme.

THE NURSING HOME

Grandma and Grandpa are
In the nursing home
Coronavirus is everywhere
And they are all alone.
Staff hiding the bodies
Too many have died
No clue what to do
Though they genuinely tried.
Hospitals are full
Where should they go
The toll of our dead
Nobody knows.
They're trying to silence
The weakest of all
The stats don't include us
Even though we too fall.
Grandma and Grandpa are
In the nursing home
Grandma's corpse is in the closet
Grandpa's in the back room.
Could you have ever imagined
Such an unthinkable doom!

PEOPLE OF COLOR

Many were sold here as slaves
Beaten and burned into graves
And now a virus is killing us
From poverty that preys.
Victims of Coronavirus
Affecting us all
But of all the deaths
It's mostly ours that do fall.
Though we're only a portion
Of the population
Most of who's dying
Are the poor of this nation.
This has been true for too long
Obviously, something's all wrong.
People of color and all people poor
Ask why death knocks
More at their door.

THE MEAT PACKERS

Almighty meat
Deemed essential for all
Even when work conditions
Cause the Reaper to call.
Coronavirus spread
Through the entire meat plant
Hundreds of hard workers
Who cry they just can't.
No staying home
The decree has been made
Work with unsafe conditions
Or never get paid.
Shoulder to shoulder
They work as one team
With no reporting
It's just not what it seems.
Meat so important
For all the U–S
The packers' lives expendable
And deemed worthless at best.
Even on the news
They may have well been called slobs
Yet they risk their own lives
For your meat and their jobs.

THE NATIVE AMERICAN

One with the earth
The Native American
Treated with little worth
Yet we're how it began.
Smallpox almost exterminated
The entire nation
And now it sadly seems
It's happening again.
A virus pandemic
Has left us all to die
With little help from this country
All I can do is just cry.
So few left of the U-S
Yet they won't send help to save
We're on our own to fight this
The Coronavirus death wave.
Where is the leader
Who must see we don't die
Piping help would be there
Was no more than a lie.
But we're still Native Americans
Though they want us to die!

THE HOMELESS

Smile, it could be worse
Is the message on my sign.
I'm homeless with Coronavirus
What a lovely time.
For us, this virus sucks
How do we quarantine?
Our home is on the streets
No room for distancing.
People call us the dirty ones
Who have no place to go.
Most don't wear a mask
They just don't care or even know.
This virus is killing us
More than this fucked-up life
Targeting the weak
With accuracy sharper than a knife.
Why does Coronavirus
Prefer to kill the poor
People of color and the homeless
Attacking them more?
Whatever, to me, this all seems too funny.
You can keep the mask
I just need some money.

THE CLEAN AIR EXPERIMENT

Planet Earth is dying
It seems mankind doesn't care
'Cause we all just stopped trying
To stay home for clean air.
For the first time clear
The air we all breathe
Proved to us so dear
When emissions did leave.
But now we're all back
No more staying at home
And yes, the clean look
Of our air is near gone.
It was proof to us all
That to clean air we can
A true wake-up call
For the preservation of man.
Covid-19 took us there
But the lessons not done
For all who do care
Truly united as one
Who remember clean air appeared
When we chose to stay home.

GEORGE FLOYD'S PANDEMIC

Most didn't know what happened
On this Covid Memorial Day.
While we honored our fallen veterans
Something horrific got away.
A man named George Floyd
Was grotesquely killed
His neck pressed by a cop's knee
For nearly nine minutes held.
Floyd's color was black
Thought to pass a fake bill
Yet the cop jumped on Floyd's neck
To press his knee for the kill.
The city now burns, even the police station
The protest of this injustice
Has spread to the entire nation.
Enough is enough of allowing the bad cop
To kill our black people
With no laws making them stop!
I can't breathe! I can't breathe!
We're sick of the lies!
No one has listened 'til now
They just left us to die!
Our masks are on
As protest has begun
And just like this virus
It won't end 'til it's won!

THE WALK

Covid-19's George Floyd
Killed by a cop
Demands police abuse
Needs to come to a stop.
Erupted with rage
Each night that did come
Masked protest to be avoided by none.
It wasn't until
George's brother did speak
That George would have wanted
To be effective yet meek.
Knees bent by even cops
Seemed this peace to reach each
Then one desperate day
The president made a vain speech
For cops to gas peaceful protesters
And make a victim of each
To clear a path for him to walk
Through his glorious breach.
Teargas clearing the way
For his photo-op day
St. Johns turned into a stage
Brandishing a Bible, with unopened page
He cried, "I'm law and order"
In front of God's temple
Spewing all should heed his call
And worship his example.

THE REOPENING

"Liberate! Liberate!" is the leader's decree
States to open from quarantine partially.
Business shutdowns have toughly hurt mine,
But is opening businesses early
Going to be the best time?
People tired from Coronavirus
Half don't even wear masks,
Yet with cases still high, they don't even ask.
To "live and let die" is the motto of the day
As we ignore this virus
And go on with our way.
To observe social distancing
I will make a new plan,
But what if this virus
Comes back raging again?
Will help be there for me
After such money's been spent?
We're already spending
What to us has been lent.
Yes, startup costs money, and the risk is so high
With only half of my customers, why do I try?
I was promised a loan that never even came
The larger businesses got it
It's always the same.
But I'm a small business of the U. S. of A.
I will rebuild again
For this is a new day!

47

UNMASKED HYPOCRISY

You can stick your rules
To follow, I'll pass.
I don't care what you say
I won't wear a mask.
They don't protect the wearer
Is what is said
So why do I care
To wear what I dread.
My job is all gone
I have no money
This Covid-19 is not funny.
Masks now required
I still don't wear one
Those weirdoes who wear them
Act like they're fun.
These masks are so hot
Making it hard to get air
It's not what I want
So why do I care.
They say people could die
If I don't wear the mask
I say let them die
It's God's will
So don't ask.

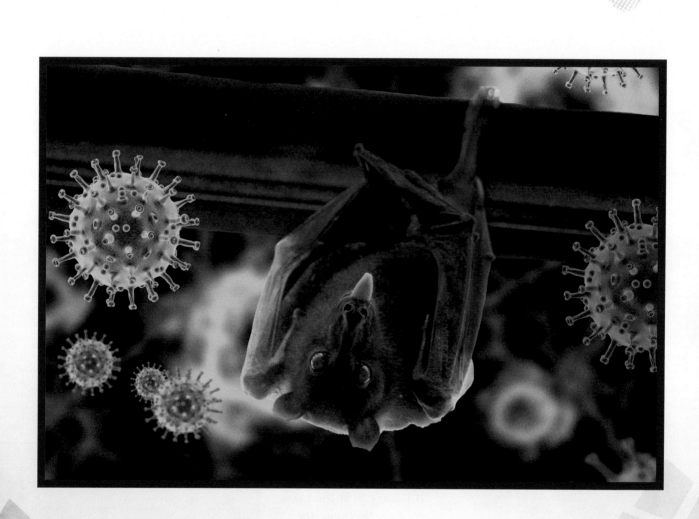

VIRUS INSIDE

Breathe deep for me
I want to go in
It's your life that I seek
Again and again.
Change positions for me
'Cause my course rearranged
No time for complacency
This game is now changed.
Go back to the start
You thought t'was the end
Plans popped by my dart
To trick, I can bend.
You must take me alone
With no one by your side
I don't hear the cries
Of souls as they die.
Breathe deeply in, Covid-19
I'm very contagious, my senses are keen.
Coronavirus, I am
Your invisible friend
With masses, I blend
And enter to win.

THE RECKONING

The world has changed
I have changed
What was the way
Has gone away.
A sunken feeling in my chest
Coronavirus here at best.
Everything has changed
Nothing's the same
All is unhinged
From this virus's game.
But though all is pained
I see a new way
So patiently, I stay
As moments pass by each day.
Things that never mattered
Now so priceless to me
My misconceptions shattered
Though isolated
I'm free.
To love with abandon
And to totally be
When actions really matter
Whether as one or as we!

THE COVID GRADUATE

The time has come for graduation
Where has it all gone, my education?
Covid-19 has changed it all
There's so much to do
So I must stand tall.
Yes, this year has been bad
No prom or sports made me sad.
Everything changed due to isolation
How will I have a real graduation?
I must rely on my creativity
To hold my graduation virtually.
A split-screen ceremony
The new normal, the way it must be.
But I am a graduate despite all of this
Leaving childhood behind
For this social abyss.
It is up to me to impact mankind
I will seek out whatever
And control what I find.
A new world awaits
It's all up to me
To graduate Covid-free
And throw my hat up with glee!

THE CAREFREE ASYMPTOMATIC

I am an asymptomatic
Covid-19 has not killed me
My freedom is problematic
But I need to just be.
I am young and invincible
No death do I fear
No graph is measurable
To the freedom I hold dear.
So die if you must
From Coronavirus
To live, I breathe lust
That kills all regardless.
The old from this die
Yet you won't see me cry
For they're the reason why
So much suffering is nigh.
So don't blame me if I live
With a selfish motive
I'm not alone
We're all young to the bone!

THE LONE PROTESTOR

George Floyd's protestors were gone
For the day they had won
I was alone
Yet felt inspired to go on.
So I made ten white signs
With multicolored pens
BLACK LIVES MATTER
This is how it began.
I taped them side by side
As drivers slowed by
Then I grabbed a big sign
And with nothing to hide
I stretched my arms high
With my sign to the sky.
Tall, white chick am I
But for this cause, I would die.
My sign waived for them all
So BLM could stand tall.
Though I was alone
Most drivers I did see
Smiled and honked or waived at me.
It was a time to show
That we all could be friends
Finally united
As our future begins!

THE FLOW

After drinking a beer
I looked where protestors would be
To see them there
But I had to pee.
Went to a park to find a restroom
Even it was locked
But I had to pee soon.
Nothing in sight, so I sucked it all in
And thought how the protestors
Must have done the same thing.
Quickly to the store
To buy the protestors some flow
Water by the case
But the cashier said no.
To sell only one bottle at a time
I cried for George Floyd
This rule is a crime.
But my food stamps will buy them
So charge me, my dear
When the old black man behind me said,
"Do you think that they'll care?"
At that moment, his pain
Showed a lifetime of wear
But I had to for the protestors
Despite his harsh glare.
The young black guy in line
As I passed by with my gift
Told me, "Good luck,"
Which was such a great lift.
Generations combined
So much to address
Yes, it's about time we heal
Racial injustice!

THE MONUMENTS

I look at your stone
And feel the stone of my heart
It chills me to the bone
Your presence tears me apart.
A monument you are
To the racist white man
After the Civil War came to its end.
You tower over me
Monuments of pure pain
Is this what I must see
Again and again?
Tear them all down
I cry from my hell
Justice rise from the ground
To break their sick spell!
Monuments topple over
No more to burn as I pass by
Just history they say
The Confederate white lie.

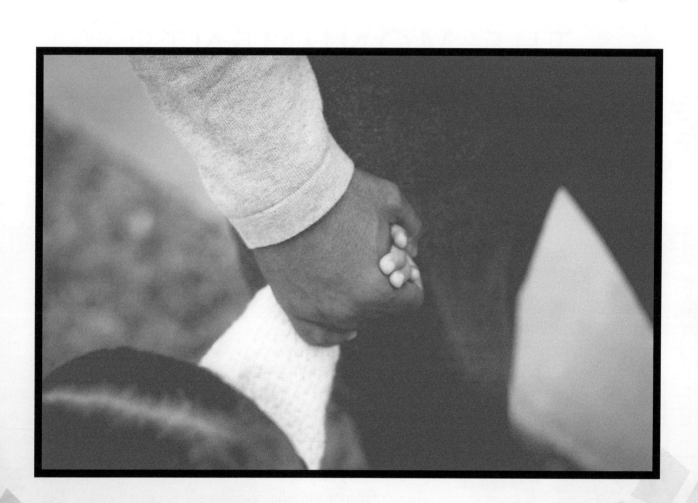

RAYSHARD BROOKS

I'm eight years old today
'Cause it's my birthday
But Daddy's gone away
We'll never get to play.
He was shot by a cop
Who wanted him to stop
But my daddy ran
'Til after two shots, he dropped.
Poor Daddy was only asleep
In the fast-food lane
Why didn't they send him home
Instead, they killed him like game.
My Daddy tried so hard
In a world that wouldn't give
He would play his only card
Trying to just live.
Always by his chair
Is where I used to sit
Now he's never there
I guess this is it.
You were supposed to be
A cop who did care
But you shot my daddy
'Til he breathed no more air.
How it hurts to know
You kicked my dad as he died
To brag that you got him
That you shot what you tried.
Every day, from now on,
I will miss my dear dad
He was everything to me
My new norm is to be sad
But my mommy and me
We also feel mad!

THE BOUNTY

My son was murdered today
And you were warned ahead
You ignored what they did say
And now my son's dead.
A year before, they warned you
That Russia planned to bounty our men
Including our women soldiers
To be killed for pure gain.
How dare you call it a hoax
That our intel did lie
It is no hoax that our soldiers have died.
You care more for a cloth flag
Than you do for our men
As long as you can brag
To you murder's no sin.
My son was a good man
And you took his life
No one should feel
The cut of this knife!

WHY

Why do you wonder why I die?
My death was likely
Even though I did try.
Coffins are piled
For the masses of dead
But first, I must gasp
From this senseless sickbed.
Graves are full from this curse
There isn't enough space
No one can keep up
With Covid-19's death pace.
Refrigerated trucks must be hauled in
To store hordes of dead
And the closest of kin.
Tears fall from my face
At the disgrace of this pain
People should not have to die
Again and again
With no family by their side
To cry for their name.
If someone allowed this
They must be insane
Don't they realize that genocide
Is not a game?

OUR CHILDREN

And a little child shall lead them
Are the words of the wise
But their suffering is an anthem
Admired by our leader's eyes.
Detained children filling each cage
Innocent children, no matter what age.
And now this travesty is to extend
Forcing children into schools
With a virus, regardless of the end.
Brain damage is a threat
To an infected child
But they're treated like some bet
As Coronavirus runs wild.
Children ever used by this evil president
For politics, they're abused
This truth's so evident.
How can people not
See the evil of this man
Must our children now be harmed
By the signature of his hand!

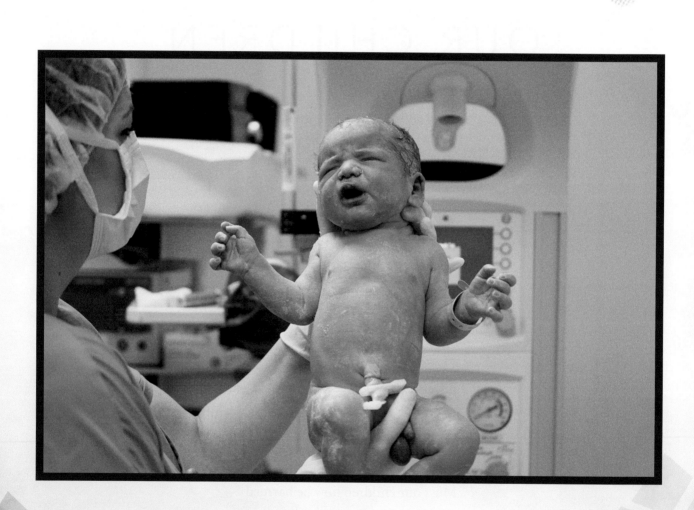

THE DELIVERY

Sweet little baby
Don't be born
Coronavirus is around us
And our masks are still on.
I'm scared to death this will get us
Your life is counting on mine
How will I keep you safe
Until it's your time.
Hospitals overflowing
No room to get in
Dear God, where will I go
When contractions begin?
911 booked due to Covid-19
Will my child be born
Without a medical team?
Contractions as expected
Starting to repeat
Knowing this virus rules
I feel looming defeat.
"Push!" the doctor says
As my baby is born
Precious life into a world
Totally torn.

Printed in the United States
By Bookmasters